W0037670

THIRTY
POLITE
THINGS
TO SAY

A Wesleyan Chapbook

THIRTY POLITE THINGS TO SAY

By Kit Reed
illustrated by Joseph Reed

WESLEYAN UNIVERSITY PRESS
Middletown, Connecticut

Wesleyan University Press
Middletown, Connecticut 06459
www.wesleyan.edu/wespress

ISBN 978-0-8195-7859-4

Thirty Polite Things to Say was first published
privately in a numbered edition of two hundred
copies in 1988. This Wesleyan chapbook was
reproduced from that edition.

Preface

With the publication of *The Book of Lobster and Forgetting*, we entered a new phase in which our friends increasingly seek advice from us about What to Do. The pressure is intense.

To meet this unprecedented demand, we have taken a new direction, in which we hope to offer specific solutions to the social puzzles posed by a changing society.

What an honor! But with honor comes responsibility. It is our duty to help our friends make their way through the thicket of contemporary problems. We must fare forward, keeping step with the times. Still we must not let standards slip. It's a narrow path we tread along the road of life. Herewith, we offer a humble first step.

There are times in the lives of us all in which we are at a loss for words. This volume attempts a partial solution.

The incidence of exclamation points suggests the level of anxiety present in our list of thoughts as to What to Do when you don't know What to Say.

1. THE INFANT GUEST

"Why no, I don't mind. I *love* children."

2. LIKE MY DRESS?

"It's you!"

3. THE HOUSEWARMING

"What distinctive taste!"

4. The Unwanted Invitation

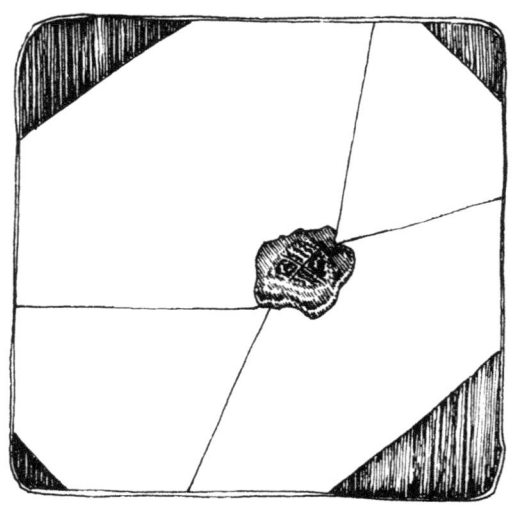

"If only we were going to be here!"

5. THE UNFORTUNATE ANNOUNCEMENT

"Divine! You're very brave."

6. THE UNEXPECTED GUEST

"Oh dear, we were just on our way out!
Pajama party down the street."

7. The Spill

"Thank heaven it's you! The *only* person
who would understand!"

8. THE UNWANTED BOOK

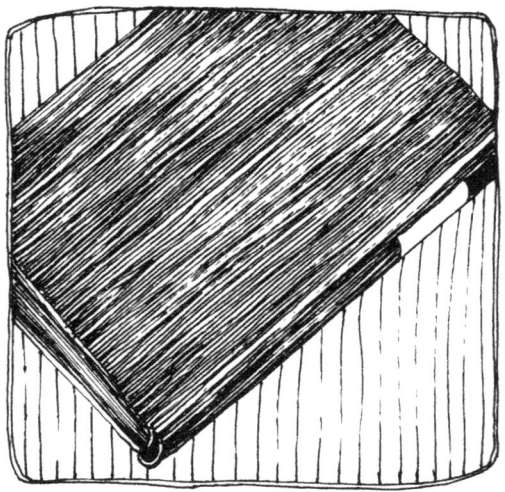

"I wanted to tell you *immediately* how thrilled
I am to have your new novel; I'll be back in
touch as soon as I've finished it."

9. THE UGLY BABY

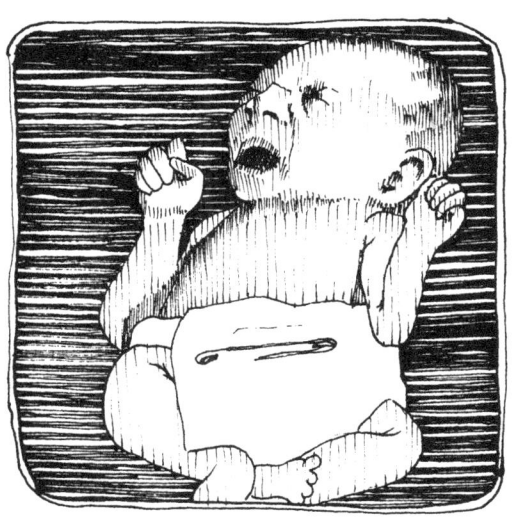

"Oooooh. Ohhhhh. Awwwww . . .
Look, a smile!"

10. The Bad Directions

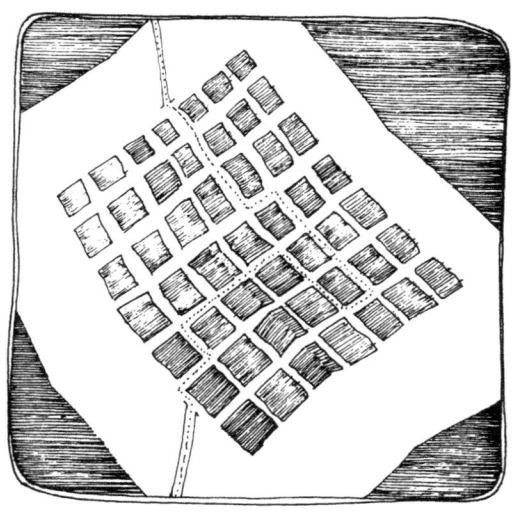

"Perfect. Everything was just as you said."

11. THE AWFUL WEEKEND

"You've been grand."

12. THE UNWANTED HEIRLOOM

"Oh, but don't you think this should be in a museum?"

13.-15. THE ALCOHOLIC PHONE CALL

"I won't keep you."

"Can I call you back? I'm waiting for an overseas call."

"Wait. Don't say another word. You have to tell X. I have X's number right here . . ."

16. THE BROKEN ANTIQUE

"Oooops . . ."

17. THE EXCRUCIATING PARTY

"There's been an accident at home.
Dispos-all, I think."

18.-20. The Bore

"Excuse me just a minute. Must be something I ate."

"Promise to wait. I'll be right back."

"Quick. Over here. There's someone I want you to meet."

21. THE VILE PET

"Smelly? No. Besides, I *love* animals."

22. THE NEW RECIPE

"Mmmmm. What did you put in it?"

23. THE UNSOLICITED MANUSCRIPT

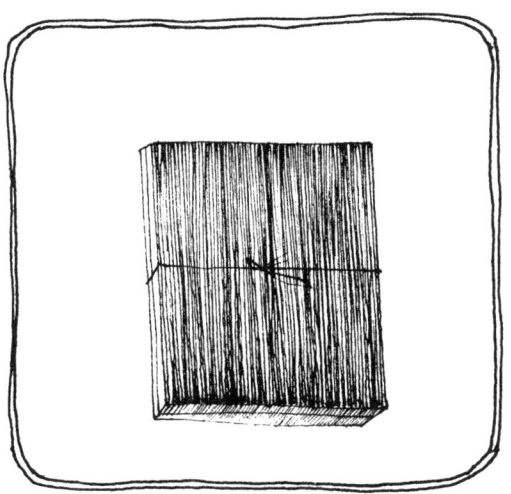

"I'm honored, but you really don't want me
to read this. You see, I have this terrible
habit of stealing good ideas . . ."

24. WHAT TO SAY TO THE ARTIST

"Ooooh. Yes. Yes!!!"

25. THE HATED AUNT

"Budapest. Tonight. We'll be in touch as
soon as we get back."

26. THE ARCH ENEMY

"How wonderful. You."

27. THE NEW HAIRDO

"What an adventurous color!"

28.-29. UNWANTED PHYSICAL CONTACT

"Oh, did I spill my drink on you?"

"Careful! Impetigo."

30. THE HYPOCHONDRIAC

"The Olingen-Knaus theory, have you heard? Talking about your symptoms makes them worse!"

Epilogue: The Unwanted Present

"Oh thank you."

Other Wesleyan Chapbooks

Kit Reed was an American author whose short stories have been nominated for the Nebula, World Fantasy, Shirley Jackson, and Tiptree Awards.

Joseph W. Reed is professor emeritus of film and American studies at Wesleyan University.

CPSIA information can be obtained
at www.ICGtesting.com
Printed in the USA
BVHW05s1929070718
520938BV00010B/38

Deaths of the Poets

A Wesleyan Chapbook

DEATHS
OF THE
POETS

by Kit Reed

designed and illustrated by Joseph Reed

WESLEYAN UNIVERSITY PRESS
Middletown, Connecticut

Wesleyan University Press
Middletown, Connecticut 06459
www.wesleyan.edu/wespress

ISBN 978-0-8195-7858-7

The Death of the Poets was first published privately in intaglio in
ten copies in 1978. This Wesleyan chapbook was reproduced from
the second, revised edition published in a limited edition of 150
copies by the author in 1991.

Deaths of the Poets
is respectfully dedicated to
(up with poets!)
RICHARD PURDY WILBUR &
(up with printers!)
HAROLD HUGO

A poet's life is like a breath
After which — you guessed it —
    DEATH.

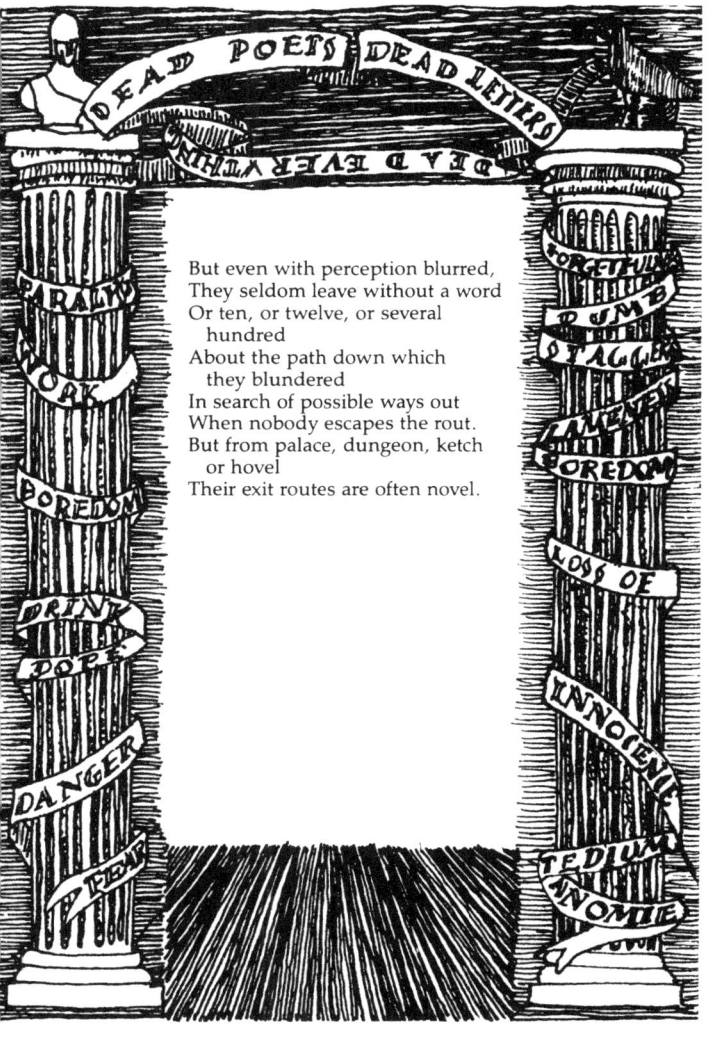

But even with perception blurred,
They seldom leave without a word
Or ten, or twelve, or several
    hundred
About the path down which
    they blundered
In search of possible ways out
When nobody escapes the rout.
But from palace, dungeon, ketch
    or hovel
Their exit routes are often novel.

Deaths of the Poets

AESCHYLUS
was taken for a rock & thus
had a turtle dashed upon his
   head
for opening. He's dead.

1

GEORGE GORDON, LORD BYRON
declined the fiery pyre on
which poor Shelley did recline
& had himself shipped home in
wine.

2

HART CRANE
took his life, it's plain:
his divine spark
was snuffed by a shark.

3

JOHN DONNE in his
  winding-sheet
thought funeral trappings neat;
in fact he quite often
dozed off in his coffin.

4

EURIPIDES
was brought to his knees
by bad reviews
(if the rumor's true).

Although MARGARET FULLER
had literary pull, her
final (if not crowning)
achievement was drowning.

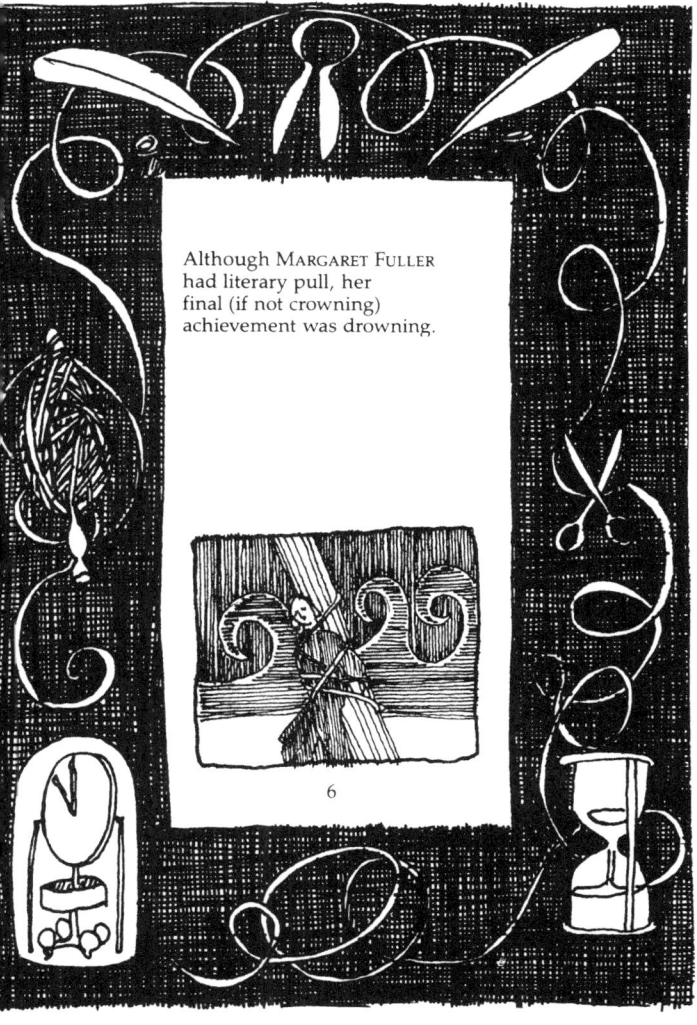

6

GOETHE, eighty-two,
ran out of things to do
&, threatened by night,
called for more light.

7

Blind HOMER,
the epic roamer,
ended his wanderings
bumping into things.

8

IKHNATON
would not be forgotten.
Fearing verse was not enough
he made the tomb of stronger
   stuff.

9

SAMUEL JOHNSON suffered
   dropsy;
when his breath began to come
   in stops, he
asked for a pillow & found it
   would do
less than he really wanted it to.

10

JOHN KEATS
in dingy sheets
spied a nightingale aloft
& contracted a cough.

11

LOVELACE in jail
grew increasingly pale;
his estates, they say,
had been whittled away.

12

MOLIERE,
a playwright with a flair,
in a rage at old age
took his last bow on stage.

13

GERARD DE NERVAL,
in love's labor's thrall,
said, Oh, what's the use
& constructed a noose.

14

DEAD POETS DEAD LETTERS

DEAD EVERYTHING

OVID, they say,
was hurried away
to exile to die.
No one knows why.

ROMA

15

DEAD POETS · DEAD LETTERS · DEAD EVERYTHING

ALEXANDER POPE,
a poet short on hope,
with potted lampreys steeped in
oil
shuffled off this mortal coil.

16

QUASIMODO, whom I once met at
  Timothy Dwight College,
was declared by the Nobel Prize
  Committee to be the fount of
  all art & knowledge.
He didn't have much to say,
but he had a funny foreign
  accent so I couldn't understand
  him anyway.

17

RILKE chose
a thorny rose
instead of a ring:
blood poisoning.

18

GEORGE SAND
dressed like a man.
She thought she looked fine,
but went into a decline.

19

For ALFRED, LORD TENNYSON
a benison over venison
was followed apace
by a fall into grace.

20

The verse of POPE URBAN
was not so unnerving
as his need to gain status
by reading them *gratis*.

21

Villon's last mile
was postponed for a while.
Three times he heard the
   headsman's knell
&, pardoned, wrote a villanelle.

22

Poor OSCAR WILDE,
a sodomite mild,
would eat like a shoat
to speed death by bloat.

23

XENOPHON
lost the will to carry on;
his death's not so drab as his
book *The Anabasis.*

24

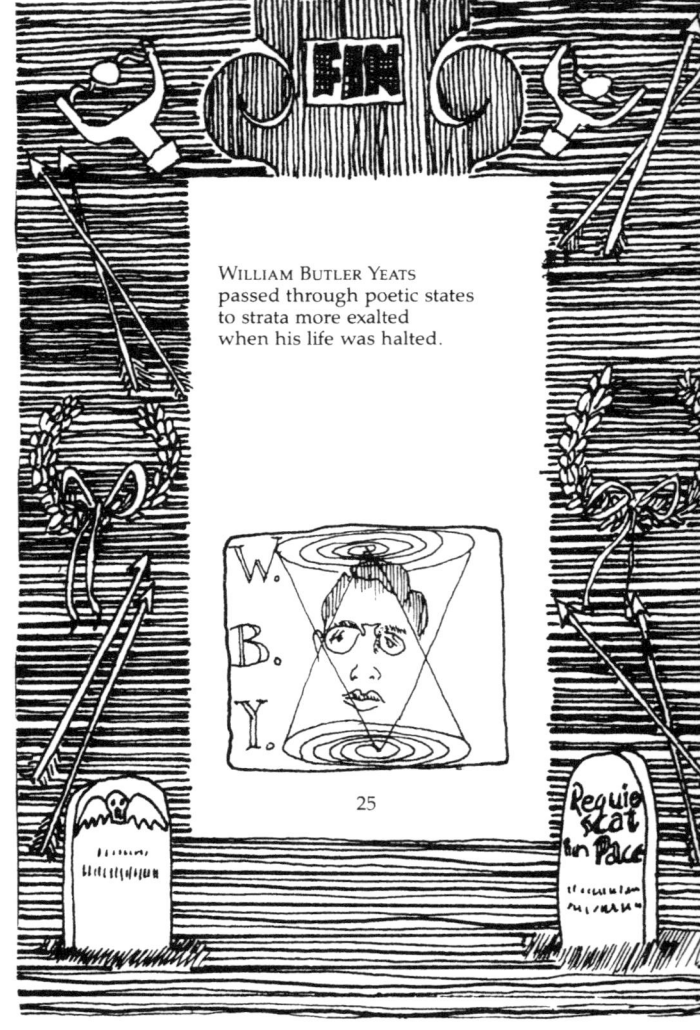

WILLIAM BUTLER YEATS
passed through poetic states
to strata more exalted
when his life was halted.

25

Zoroaster wasn't a poet
& we know it
but we think it's safe to say
he died anyway.

26

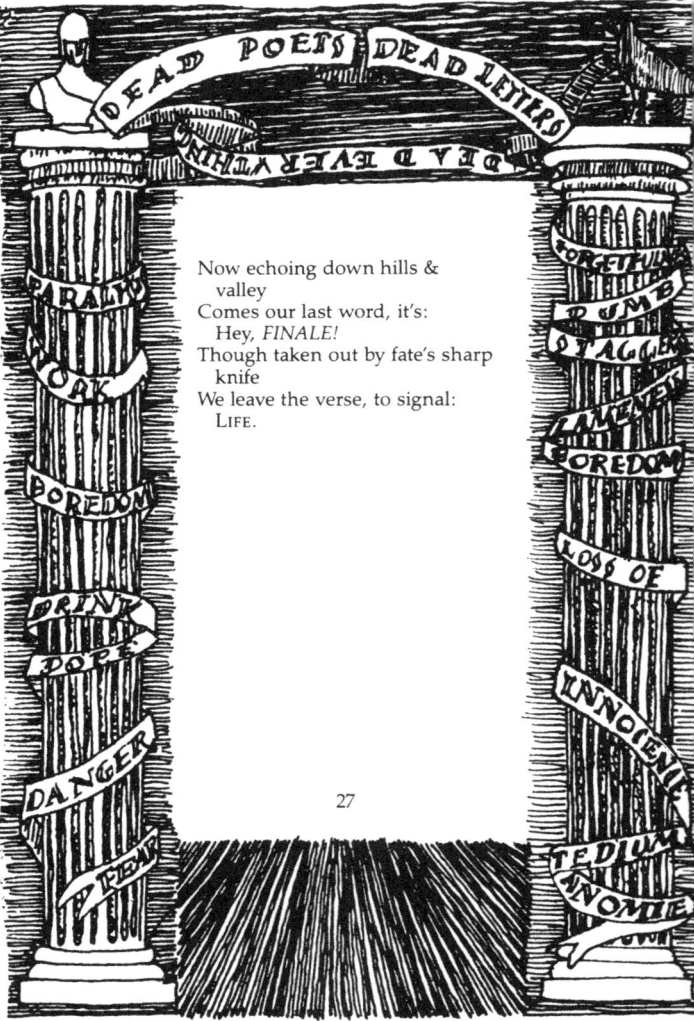

DEAD POETS DEAD LETTERS
DEAD EVERYTHING

Now echoing down hills &
   valley
Comes our last word, it's:
   Hey, *FINALE!*
Though taken out by fate's sharp
   knife
We leave the verse, to signal:
   LIFE.

27

KIT REED was an American author whose short stories have been nominated for the Nebula, World Fantasy, Shirley Jackson, and Tiptree Awards.

JOSEPH W. REED is professor emeritus of film and American studies at Wesleyan University.

CPSIA information can be obtained
at www.ICGtesting.com
Printed in the USA
BVHW02s2259090718
520938BV00010B/2/378

9 780819 578587

dog
truths

A Wesleyan Chapbook

dog
truths

by kit reed

illustrations and design by joseph reed

wesleyan university press

middletown, connecticut

Wesleyan University Press
Middletown, Connecticut 06459
www.wesleyan.edu/wespress

ISBN 978-0-8195-7860-0

Dog Truths was first published privately in a numbered edition in
1996. This Wesleyan chapbook was reproduced from the second
hors commerce edition.

being a refutation of Certain Base Canards

and a Setting of the Record Straight

in the matter of the Scottish Terrier

as measured against other breeds

based on close observation

by experts

In a Position to Know

dog
truths

What Kind of Dog Are You Getting? Behavior Profiles

When 96 dog experts were asked to rate the 56 most common breeds of purebred dogs, the tally gave an idea of where individual breeds stand in 13 characteristics, from the top 10 percent to the bottom 10 percent.

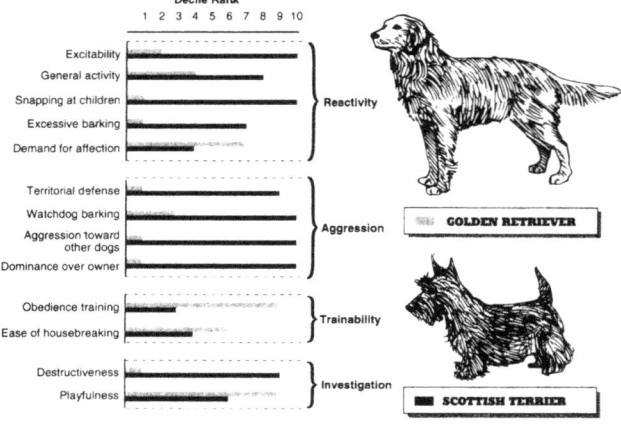

Decile Rank
1 2 3 4 5 6 7 8 9 10

Reactivity
- Excitability
- General activity
- Snapping at children
- Excessive barking
- Demand for affection

Aggression
- Territorial defense
- Watchdog barking
- Aggression toward other dogs
- Dominance over owner

Trainability
- Obedience training
- Ease of housebreaking

Investigation
- Destructiveness
- Playfulness

GOLDEN RETRIEVER

SCOTTISH TERRIER

Source: "The Perfect Puppy," B. L. and L. A. Hart (W. H. Freeman & Company)

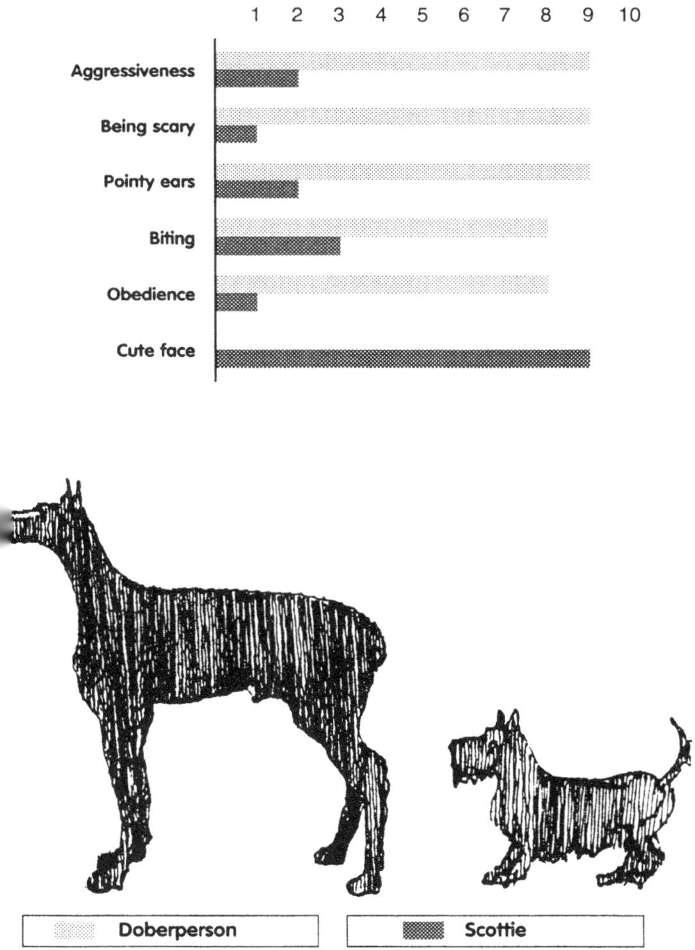

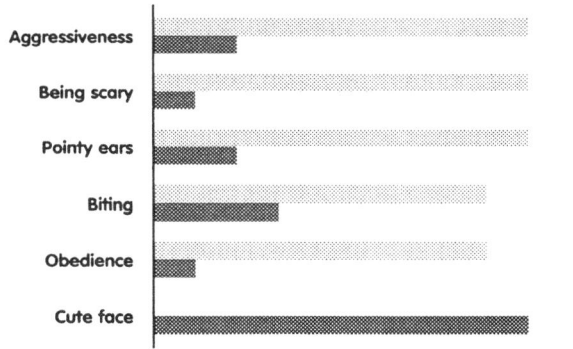

	1	2	3	4	5	6	7	8	9	10
Aggressiveness										
Being scary										
Pointy ears										
Biting										
Obedience										
Cute face										

Doberperson

Scottie

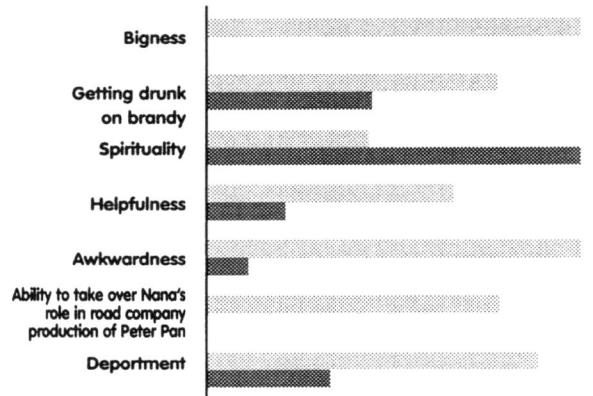

	1	2	3	4	5	6	7	8	9	10

Bigness

Getting drunk on brandy

Spirituality

Helpfulness

Awkwardness

Ability to take over Nana's role in road company production of Peter Pan

Deportment

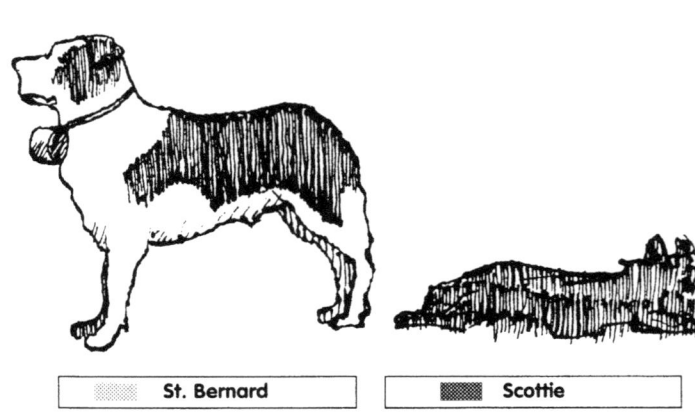

| St. Bernard | Scottie |

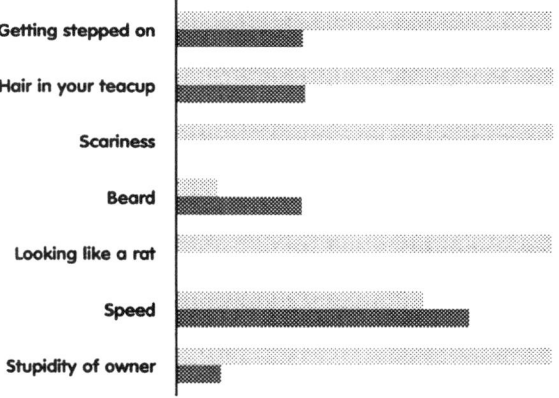

| | 1 | 2 | 3 | 4 | 5 | 6 | 7 | 8 | 9 | 10 |

Getting stepped on

Hair in your teacup

Scariness

Beard

Looking like a rat

Speed

Stupidity of owner

| | Chihuahua | | | Scottie |

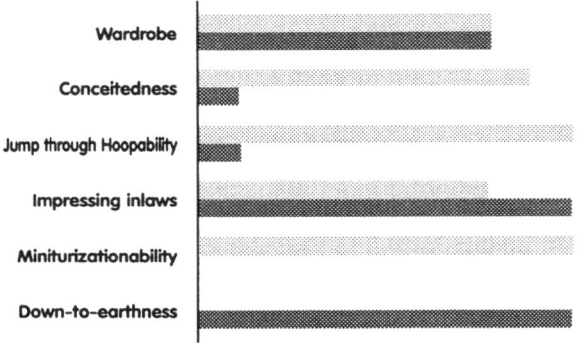

| | 1 | 2 | 3 | 4 | 5 | 6 | 7 | 8 | 9 | 10 |

Wardrobe

Conceitedness

Jump through Hoopability

Impressing inlaws

Miniturizationability

Down-to-earthness

Poodle

Scottie

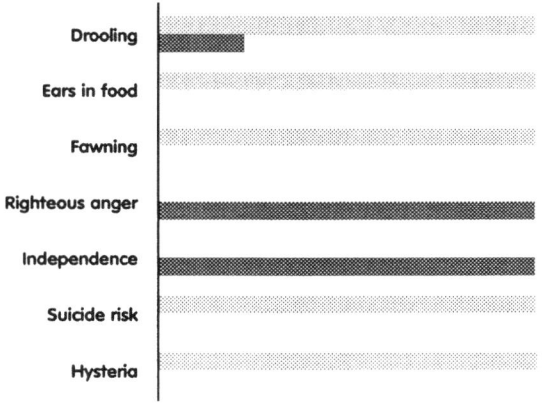

	1	2	3	4	5	6	7	8	9	10
Drooling										
Ears in food										
Fawning										
Righteous anger										
Independence										
Suicide risk										
Hysteria										

|  Cocker Spaniel | Scottie |

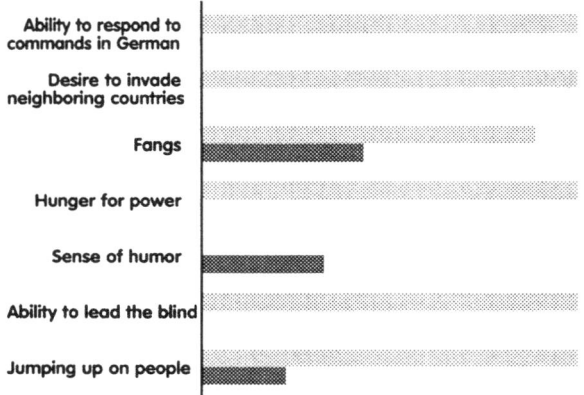

	1	2	3	4	5	6	7	8	9	10

Ability to respond to commands in German

Desire to invade neighboring countries

Fangs

Hunger for power

Sense of humor

Ability to lead the blind

Jumping up on people

German Shepherd aka
Alsatian aka
Belgian Police Dog

Scottie

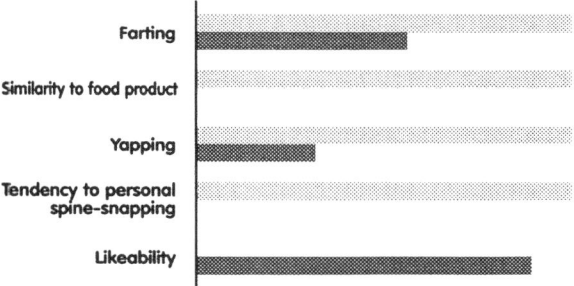

	1 2 3 4 5 6 7 8 9 10
Farting	
Similarity to food product	
Yapping	
Tendency to personal spine-snapping	
Likeability	

Dachshund

Scottie

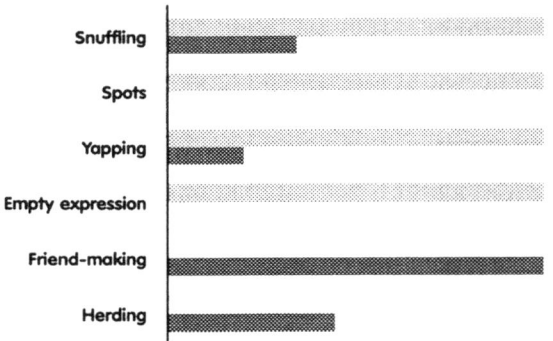

	1	2	3	4	5	6	7	8	9	10

Snuffling

Spots

Yapping

Empty expression

Friend-making

Herding

Boston Bull

Scottie

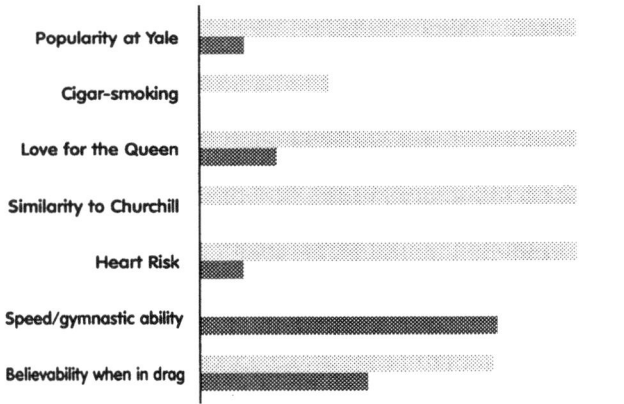

| | 1 | 2 | 3 | 4 | 5 | 6 | 7 | 8 | 9 | 10 |

Popularity at Yale

Cigar-smoking

Love for the Queen

Similarity to Churchill

Heart Risk

Speed/gymnastic ability

Believability when in drag

| English Bulldog | Scottie |

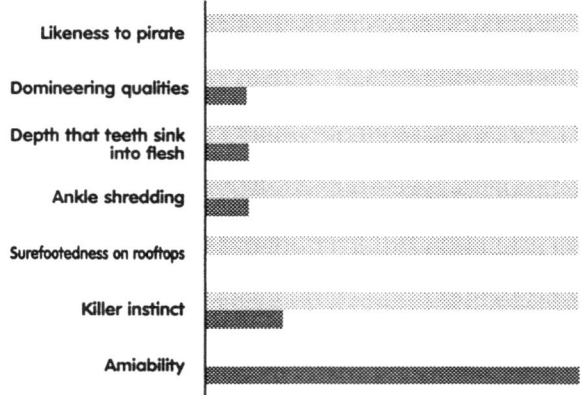

	1	2	3	4	5	6	7	8	9	10

- Likeness to pirate
- Domineering qualities
- Depth that teeth sink into flesh
- Ankle shredding
- Surefootedness on rooftops
- Killer instinct
- Amiability

Bull Terrier

Scottie

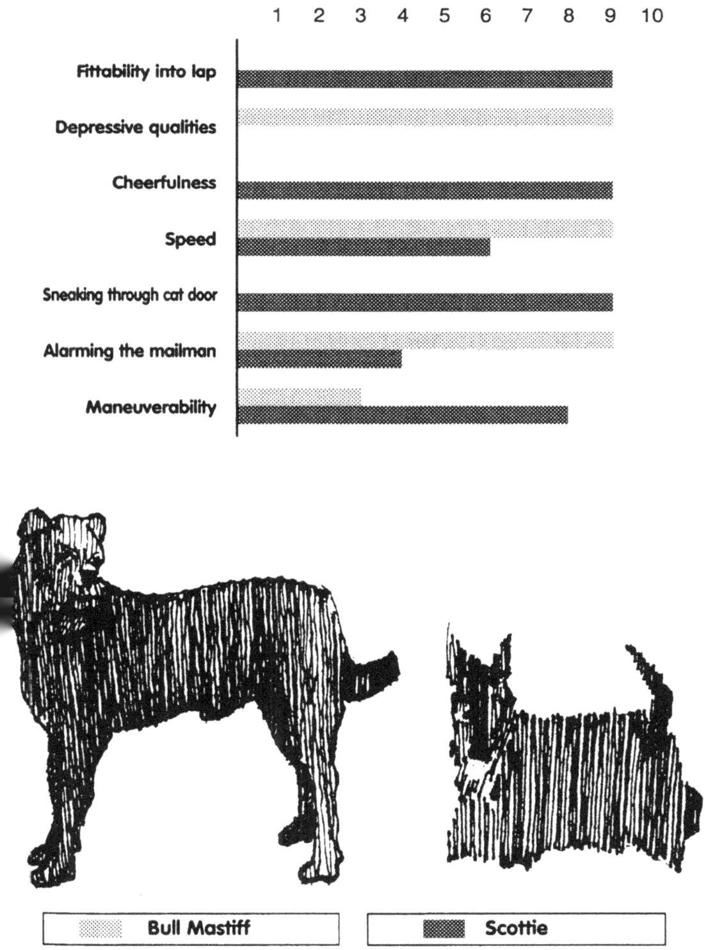

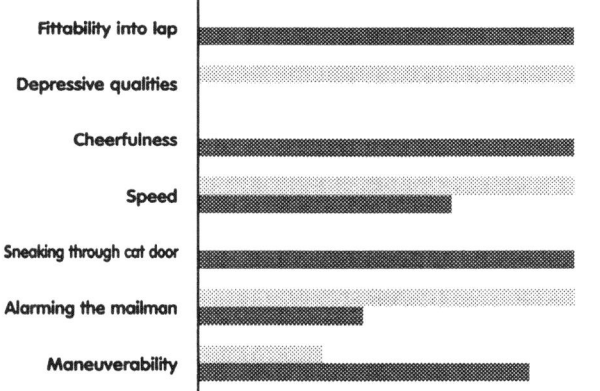

	1	2	3	4	5	6	7	8	9	10

Fittability into lap

Depressive qualities

Cheerfulness

Speed

Sneaking through cat door

Alarming the mailman

Maneuverability

| Bull Mastiff | Scottie |

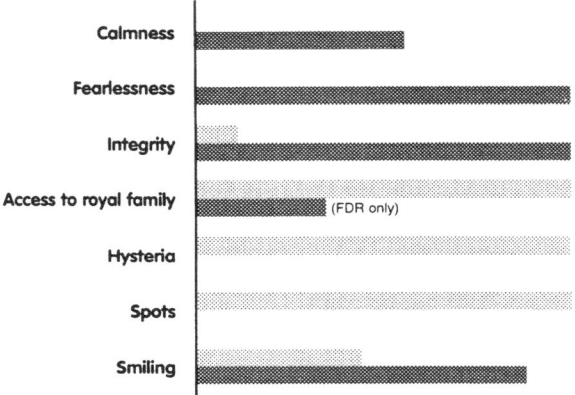

	1	2	3	4	5	6	7	8	9	10
Calmness										
Fearlessness										
Integrity										
Access to royal family			(FDR only)							
Hysteria										
Spots										
Smiling										

 King Charles Spaniel   Scottie

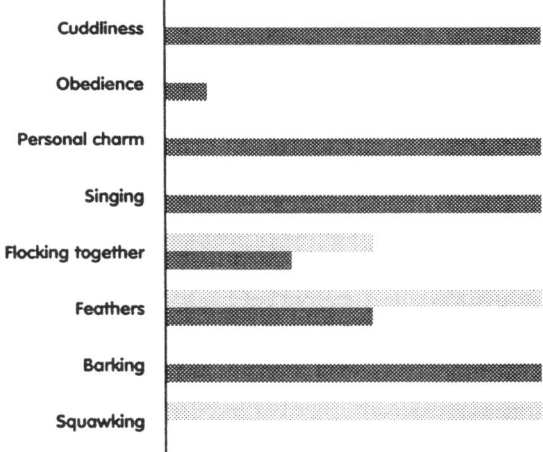

	1	2	3	4	5	6	7	8	9	10

Cuddliness

Obedience

Personal charm

Singing

Flocking together

Feathers

Barking

Squawking

| Budgerigar | Scottie |

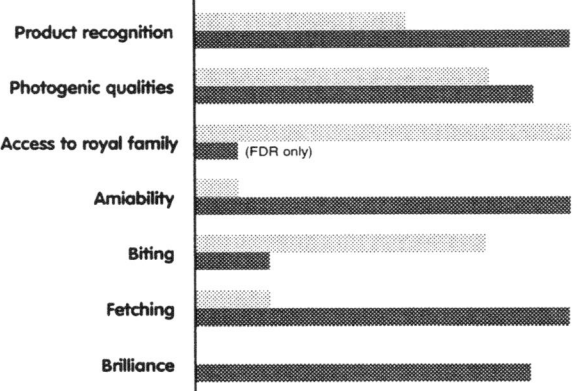

	1	2	3	4	5	6	7	8	9	10

Product recognition

Photogenic qualities

Access to royal family (FDR only)

Amiability

Biting

Fetching

Brilliance

Corgi	Scottie

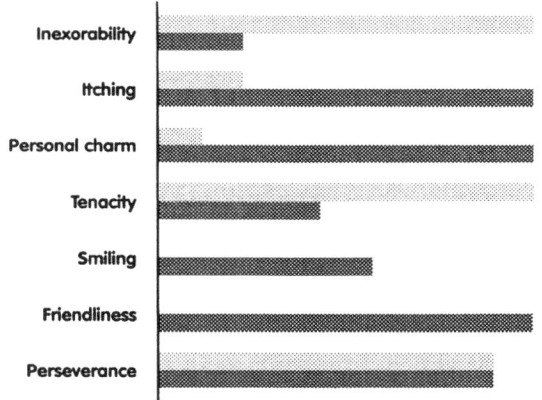

	1	2	3	4	5	6	7	8	9	10
Inexorability										
Itching										
Personal charm										
Tenacity										
Smiling										
Friendliness										
Perseverance										

	1	2	3	4	5	6	7	8	9	10

Agility

Obedience

Personal beauty

Charm

Interest in food

Interest in sex

Interest in people

Duff

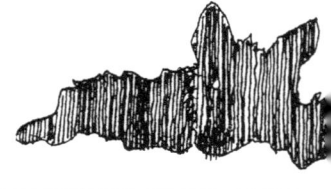

Asta

Other Wesleyan Chapbooks

Entanglements
Rae Armantrout

*I Will Teach You about Murder:
29 Love Poems*
edited by Shea Fitzpatrick,
Sallie Fullerton, and Torii Johnson

Thirty Polite Things to Say
Kit Reed
illustrations by Joseph W. Reed

Deaths of the Poets
Kit Reed
illustrations by Joseph W. Reed

Kit Reed was an American author whose short stories have been nominated for the Nebula, World Fantasy, Shirley Jackson, and Tiptree Awards.

Joseph W. Reed is professor emeritus of film and American studies at Wesleyan University.

CPSIA information can be obtained
at www.ICGtesting.com
Printed in the USA
BVHW05s1929070718
520938BV00011B/89/P